W9-CKM-536

FARM ANIMALS

LIFE ON THE FARM

Lynn M. Stone

Rourke Publishing LLC
Vero Beach, Florida 32964

www.rourkepublishing.com

PHOTO CREDITS:
All photos © Lynn M. Stone

EDITORIAL SERVICES:
Pamela Schroeder

Library of Congress Cataloging-in-Publication Data

Stone, Lynn M.
    Farm Animals / Lynn M. Stone
        p. cm. — (Life on the farm)
    Summary: Briefly discusses farms that raise domestic animals such as beef
    cattle, sheeps, hogs, chickens, and turkeys as livestock.
    ISBN 1-58952-090-4
     1. Livestock—Juvenile literature. [1. Livestock. 2. Farm Animals. 3. Farms.]
    I. Title

SF75.5 .S76 2001
636—dc21   2001032667

Printed in the USA

TABLE OF CONTENTS

FARM ANIMALS

Many North American farmers raise animals. Farmers raise animals for meat, milk, eggs, and wool. Farmers sell these **products** to earn a living. **Beef** cattle, sheep, hogs, and chickens supply most of these products.

Long ago, American farmers used some kinds of farm animals to do farm work. Working farm animals are not often used now.

Farmers raise beef cattle, like this Hereford in Wisconsin, for their meat.

5

Most modern animal farms raise one kind of animal for sale. A **dairy** farm raises cattle that give large amounts of milk. A dairy farmer is not likely to raise sheep or hogs, too.

Farm animals are also called **domestic** animals, or **livestock**. Farmers have raised domestic animals for thousands of years. Domestic animals are much tamer than their wild cousins. They are used to being around people.

This female, or nanny, goat is part of a dairy goat herd.

The most common farm animals are cattle, horses, sheep, hogs, chickens, and turkeys. A few farmers in North America raise goats, donkeys, rabbits, mules, ducks, geese, and guinea fowl.

Farmers raise many **breeds** of each kind of farm animal. Each breed is a little different than the others. The Holstein breed of dairy cattle, for example, gives more milk than other cattle breeds.

The Guernsey cow here gives less milk than a Holstein cow, but the Guernsey's milk is creamier.

CATTLE

Many dairy cattle are raised on small, family-owned farms. Most cows on dairy farms are female. Female cows give us milk and cream. Milk and cream can be made into butter, ice cream, cheese, and yogurt.

Most beef cattle are raised on big ranches in Florida or the West. Beef cattle are used for meat.

These longhorn beef cattle live on a Texas ranch.

An Iowa blue breed rooster crows on a poultry farm.

Tolouse geese parade across a pasture they share with dairy goats.

HORSES

Before cars and tractors, people needed horses. People rode horses from place to place. **Draft** horses plowed fields and pulled wagons and sleighs.

Farmers today raise horses mostly to ride for fun. A few farmers still use draft horses to pull or plow.

Draft horses are heavier than riding horses. They have stronger, thicker legs, too.

This rare Lipizzan stallion is a highly-trained riding horse.

HOGS

Farmers raise hogs for their meat. Bacon and ham are two of the meat products from hogs.

Farmers raise hogs in pens, either indoors or outdoors. Pigs outdoors like to stay in mud pools. They also like to poke their **snouts** into soil to find food. Hogs eat mostly corn and grain, as most farm animals do.

Hog Heaven. A female pig, called a sow, cools off in a mud bath.

SHEEP AND GOATS

Sheep are raised for both meat and wool. Wool is the thick, warm hair that covers sheep.

Mother sheep are called **ewes**. They sometimes have twins or triplets. Their babies are called lambs.

Goats are close cousins of sheep. Most North American goat farmers raise goats for milk and goat cheese. Young goats are called kids.

A day-old lamb already wears a blanket of light wool.

POULTRY

Birds raised on farms are called **poultry**. The most common kinds of poultry in North America are chickens and turkeys.

Farmers raise chickens for meat and the eggs they lay. Turkeys, ducks, and geese are raised for meat alone.

A Narragansett tom turkey fans its tail feathers for turkey hens.

Farm birds can be raised indoors or outdoors. Big chicken farms raise their birds in long barns.

Turkeys are the biggest farm birds. They sometimes weigh more than 40 pounds (18 kilograms). Most turkeys, though, are sent to market when they weigh just 12 to 24 pounds (5.5 to 11 kg).

Not all poultry farmers sell meat or eggs. Some chicken farmers raise old or fancy breeds to show.

GLOSSARY

beef (BEEF) — the meat of cattle

breed (BREED) — within a kind of domestic animal, one special type, such as Holstein cattle

dairy (DAYR ee) — having to do with milking cows, milk, and milk products

domestic (deh MES tik) — having to do with animals of the home or farm

draft (DRAFT) — used for pulling loads

ewe (YOO) — adult female sheep

livestock (LYV stahk) — farm animals

poultry (POHL tree) — birds raised on farms, especially chickens, turkeys, ducks, and geese

product (PRAHD ekt) — that which is made or produced

snout (SNOWT) — the nose of an animal, especially a pig's

INDEX

Further Reading

Cooper, Jason. *Goats*, Rourke, 1995.
Stone, Lynn M. *Chickens*. Rourke, 1990.
Stone, Lynn M. *Cows*. Rourke, 1990.

Websites To Visit

www.albc-usa.org
www.fortunecity.com

About The Author

Lynn Stone is the author of more than 400 children's books. He is a talented natural history photographer as well. Lynn, a former teacher, travels worldwide to photograph wildlife in its natural habitat.